REBUILDING
THE TEMPLE AT
JERUSALEM

REBUILDING
THE TEMPLE AT
JERUSALEM

THE PERSIAN EMPIRE'S INFLUENCE IN
THE REBUILDING OF JERUSALEM

SANDY MILLER

Copyright © 2021 Sandy Miller.

All rights reserved. No part of this book may be reproduced in any form or by any electronic or mechanical means, including information storage and retrieval systems, without permission in writing from the publisher, except by reviewers, who may quote brief passages in a review.

ISBN: 978-1-956515-68-8 (Paperback Edition)
ISBN: 978-1-956515-69-5 (Hardcover Edition)
ISBN: 978-1-956515-67-1 (E-book Edition)

Library of Congress Control Number: 2021918506

Scripture taken from the HOLY BIBLE, NEW INTERNATIONAL VERSION, Copyright 1973, 1978, 1984 by International Bible Society. Used by permission of Zondervan. All rights reserved.

Scripture taken from the Holy Bible, New International Version Archaeological Study Bible, by Zondervan, Copyright 2005 by the Zondervan Corporation. Used by permission of Zondervan. All rights reserved.

Scripture taken from the Holy Bible, New International Version, Copyright 1973, 1978, 1984, by International Bible Society. Used by permission of Zondervan. All rights reserved.

Apocrypha writings taken from New Revised Standard Version Bible with Apocrypha, Copyright 1989, by the division of Christian Education of the National Council of the Churches of Christ in the United States of America. Used by permission. All rights reserved.

Readings taken from the New Testament and Psalms, An Inclusive Version, Copyright 1995, by Oxford University Press, Inc. Used by permission. All rights reserved.

Graphic (Visions of Daniel), Page 1301; taken from New International Version Study Bible edited by Kenneth L. Barker; (ISBN 9780310925705).

Book Ordering Information

Phone Number: 315 288-7939 ext. 1000 or 347-901-4920
Email: info@globalsummithouse.com
Global Summit House
www.globalsummithouse.com

Printed in the United State of America

Contents

Introduction ix

Lecture 1: The Babylonian King Nebuchadnezzar 1

Lecture 2: The Image of Gold and the Fiery Furnace 11

Lecture 3: Nebuchadnezzar's Strange Malady 16

Lecture 4: The Persian World Empire 25

Lecture 5: Cyrus the Great Decrees that Jewish Exiles
May Return to Jerusalem to Rebuild the Temple 33

Lecture 6: Cambyses's Brief Reign Followed by Darius I 40

Lecture 7: Xerxes's Only Connection to the
Rebuilding of Jerusalem 51

Lecture 8: King Artaxerxes I Sends Nehemiah to
Rebuild Jerusalem 57

Conclusion 71

Bibliography 73

To the Center for Lifelong Learning on the campus of the University of West Florida-Northwest Florida State College and my students, for giving me the opportunity to teach the Bible as literature there for more than eleven years. Feedback in class discussions has enlightened and encouraged me to keep studying this fascinating book. I always look forward to teaching the Bible as literature because nobody learns more than the teacher. *Rebuilding the Temple at Jerusalem* is the result of that kind of teaching opportunity.

Introduction

Over the past seventeen years, I have taught the Bible as Cultural Literature at the Center for Lifelong Learning on the shared campus of the University of West Florida/Northwest Florida State College in Ft. Walton Beach, Florida as well as Florida Gulf Coast Academy in Naples, Florida.

Teaching the Bible as Literature approaches the Bible as it would a piece of literature such as the Qur'an. Even though the Bible and the Qur'an are both sacred to worshippers of their faiths, their scriptures can often be set in a time frame ruled by historical kings who left archaeological records and artifacts that often validate the accuracy of the culture's sacred writings.

Encyclopedias of mythology containing information about gods and goddesses of the Middle East are used in this kind of study. Understanding the mythologies through scholarly articles about fertility rites, male and female temple prostitutes, and animal and human sacrifice makes it easy to understand why the God of Israel forbade idol worship. Ancient history, archaeology, mythology, records of ancient church fathers, ancient records of cultural laws, and medical and psychological discoveries all shed light on scriptures whose meanings have been lost through time.

Studying Ezra and Nehemiah for a new Bible as Literature class, I found Cyrus the Great, founder of the Persian Empire, instigated the reconstruction of the temple at Jerusalem, which had been destroyed by Nebuchadnezzar and the Babylonian Empire. Then I discovered that Isaiah's prophecies (740–700

BCE), before the fall of Jerusalem, had predicted that Jerusalem would be destroyed and that someone named Cyrus would order that the temple be rebuilt. Isaiah prophesied: "This is what the Lord says…of Cyrus, 'He is my shepherd and will accomplish all that I please; he will say of Jerusalem, "Let it be rebuilt," and of the temple, "Let its foundations be laid."(Isaiah 44:24a–28 NIV)

Eager to find out more, I conducted research that revealed several Persian kings were involved in the restoration of the Promised Land of the Jews. The Persian Empire was in power for more than two hundred years, so I had to get those kings straight. Since the media often include news about Iran, which is modern-day Persia, that made my study doubly interesting. Daniel, Nehemiah, Ezra, Haggai, Zechariah, and Esther all lived during the time of the Persian Empire and were involved with various Persian kings. Integrating books of the Bible with ancient history, mythology, archaeology, and cultural history brought the restoration of the temple to life for me. As a bonus, my students liked the class!

As you move through the pages of *Rebuilding the Temple at Jerusalem*, which follows 114 years of the Persian Empire, I think you too will enjoy the journey. It is a story of Persian kings who helped various Bible figures preserve the Promised Land for future generations. The Bible figures were Old Testament people who kept records of their efforts on behalf of Jerusalem. Stories of their unique involvement with the Persian Empire are found in the Old Testament books that bear their names: Daniel, Haggai, Zechariah, Ezra, Nehemiah, and Esther.

LECTURE 1

The Babylonian King Nebuchadnezzar

Welcome, students of the Bible. We will be using many versions of the Bible as the text for *Rebuilding the Temple at Jerusalem*. You can follow in any Bible you have, even though the language may be slightly different. The *New International Version Archaeological Study Bible* was my guide as I prepared these lectures, because it has up-to-date footnotes and articles that make the text so much clearer. A copy of this version is available from Amazon.com.

Daniel was a Hebrew prince who was among the first people to be deported by the Babylonian Empire, even before the destruction of Jerusalem. Daniel and his three young friends—who were probably also from the royal family—were exiled early in the Babylonian campaign to keep them from causing trouble for the conquering power.

Since these young people were familiar with palace life and were knowledgeable about Jewish customs, they could be very useful to Nebuchadnezzar as he ruled the Babylonian Empire. For three years, eighteen-year-old Daniel and Shadrach, Meshach, and Abednego were trained in Babylonian language, culture, and literature to ready them to serve King Nebuchadnezzar in the royal court.

Meanwhile, Nebuchadnezzar continued to chip away at Jerusalem. Because of King Hezekiah's earlier preparation of an underground water tunnel, Jerusalem was able to withstand these punishing sieges. King Jehoiakim, Israel's puppet ruler, pledged his support to Nebuchadnezzar rather than fight the Babylonian army. When he did rebel, Babylonian, Aramean, Moabite and Ammonite raiders harassed Jerusalem.

In 597 BCE, Nebuchadnezzar entered Jerusalem and captured 18 year old King Jehoiachin who had replaced his father as king. Babylonian records state that Nebuchadnezzar "encamped against the city of Judah…seized the city and captured the king." He also looted the palace of its royal trappings and the temple of its golden ceremonial cups as spoils of war. King Jehoiachin, the royal family, and 10,000 of Jerusalem's leaders were deported (Footnote to II Ki. 24:10-12, NIVASB).

Zedekiah became the last king of Israel but he too rebelled. The final siege of Jerusalem lasted two and a half years before Babylon finally sent troops to torch Jerusalem and level the city walls. Zedekiah fled but was captured. "They killed the sons of Zedekiah before his eyes. Then they put out his eyes, bound him with bronze shackles and took him to Babylon."(II Ki.25:7, NIV)

DISCUSSION QUESTIONS

1. Why would Babylon go to the trouble of taking captives to Babylon instead of leaving conquered people in their decimated cities? (See 2 Ki.24:14-16)

2. Who do you think would be selected for exile, and who would be left to live in the ruined cities of Judah? (See 2 Ki. 24:14-16)

3. Why do you think all the people with status were deported?

Daniel served King Nebuchadnezzar in the palace at Babylon and was still there when the Persians invaded nearly seventy years later. Ruins from that ancient city are about twenty miles from today's city of Baghdad, Iraq.

Through several deportations, Jewish exiles, including the prophet Ezekiel, were settled near the Kebar River, which is thought to have been a canal off the Euphrates. They lived there, built houses, farmed the land, and had businesses. Many became prosperous enough that when Cyrus the Persian conquered Babylon and decreed that all exiles might return to Judah, many decided to stay in Babylon.

Our first reading is from Daniel 2. During the second year of Nebuchadnezzar's reign, the king had a dream that troubled him, so he called in the magicians, enchanters, sorcerers, and astrologers to help him interpret the dream. Daniel was one of the group of wise men the king engaged to solve mysteries that required abilities which we today call extrasensory perception.

The biggest problem was that the king did not remember his dream. The wise men did not know how to deal with this. All of the group the king summoned insisted only the gods could tell the king what he had dreamed; no magician, astrologer or enchanter on earth could tell the king what he had dreamed. King Nebuchadnezzar was furious! "The king replied to the astrologers, 'This is what I have firmly decided, if you do not tell me what my dream was and interpret it, I will have you cut you in pieces and your houses turned into piles of rubble.'" (Daniel 2:5 NIVASB)

Dismissing them, he immediately decreed that all wise men be put to death. Men came looking for Daniel and his friends to deliver them to the executioner.

Discussion Questions

1. From our story so far, what kind of a king do you think Nebuchadnezzar was? (Opinion of the reader)
2. Daniel was a deportee or exile from a conquered nation. How important, do you think, this Judean captive prince was to King Nebuchadnezzar? (Probably unimportant)
3. What do you think it would have been like to be in Daniel's place as one of the wise men who serve the king?
4. What has the king decided is Daniel's fate now? (See Dan. 2:5)
5. Was King Nebuchadnezzar a historical ruler?

When Daniel heard about the decree, he spoke to the commander of the king's guard and found the order had already been given to execute all astrologers, magicians, and fortune-tellers. Daniel went to the king and asked for time to ask his God to help him interpret Nebuchadnezzar's dreams. Then Daniel and his friends prayed to their God for help and mercy so he and all of his friends would not be executed. During the night Daniel's God revealed the king's dream and its interpretation to Daniel in a vision. The king's executioner brought Daniel to Nebuchadnezzar to tell him his dream and interpret it.

Brusquely asking Daniel if he had come because he was able to tell him what his dream was and interpret it, Daniel replied that no wise man, enchanter, or diviner could tell the king what he had dreamed. Nevertheless, the God Daniel worshipped was a revealer of mysteries. Continuing, he told him that through his dream King Nebuchadnezzar received a revelation of what was to come in the days ahead. Daniel's God revealed the mystery so the king could understand what was in his mind.

In your dream, you saw a large statue—an enormous, dazzling statue, awesome in appearance. The head of the statue was made of pure gold, its chest and arms of silver, its belly and thighs of bronze, its legs of iron, its feet partly of iron and partly of baked clay. While you were watching, a rock was cut out, but not by human hands. It struck the statue on its feet of iron and clay and smashed them. Then the iron, the clay, the bronze, the silver and the gold were broken to pieces at the same time and became like chaff on a threshing floor in the summer. The wind swept them away without leaving a trace. The rock that struck the statue became a large mountain and filled the whole earth." (Daniel 2:31b–35 NIVASB)

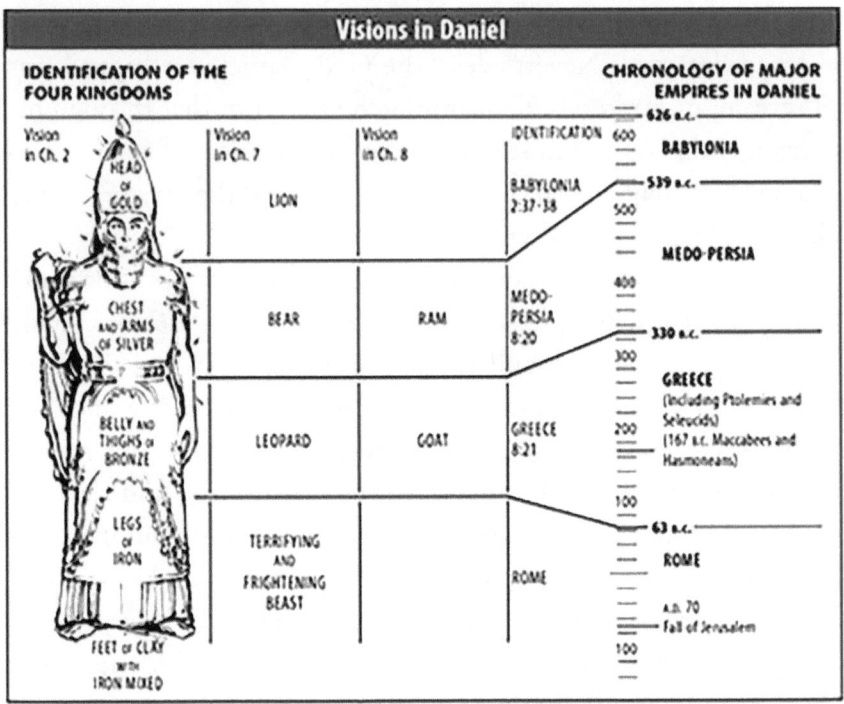

Graphic taken from the Holy Bible, New International Version. Copyright 1973, 1978, 1984 by International Bible Society. Used by permission of Zondervan Publishing House. All rights reserved.

You can follow this paraphrase of the interpretation of Nebuchadnezzar's dream in any version of the Bible in the book of Daniel, Chapter 2.

Then Daniel unfolded the interpretation. The God of heaven has made you the ruler over all mankind, all beasts and birds on the entire earth. You control everything that lives and moves. You are the head of pure gold that you saw in your dream.

After your time to rule is over, another kingdom will come to rule the whole earth, but this rule will be inferior, not of pure gold as is yours. In your dream, the statue you saw indicated this by its arms and chest of silver. Then a third kingdom will have dominion over the earth. This reign was symbolized by the statue's belly and thighs made of bronze.

Finally, a fourth king will take over the earth, strong as iron—moving over the earth and breaking the others to pieces, as iron smashes everything. The feet and toes were mixed of baked clay and iron because it will be a divided kingdom; yet in places it will have the strength of iron. As the toes showed by being partly iron and partly clay, so this kingdom will be somewhat strong but also brittle. Just so, the people will not be united, for iron does not mix with clay.

During the reign of those kings, the God of heaven will create a kingdom that will never end nor be taken over by others. All other kingdoms will end, as they will be broken by the power of this heavenly kingdom. This will be an eternal kingdom that will endure forever. The meaning of the rock hewn out of a mountain which smashed the iron, the bronze, the clay, the silver, and the gold kingdoms has shown you, King Nebuchadnezzar, what is to take place. Your vision is true, and its interpretation is worthy of trust. King Nebuchadnezzar prostrated himself before Daniel and honored him with offerings, gifts, and incense. "The king said to Daniel, 'Surely your God is the God of gods and the Lord of kings and a revealer of mysteries, for you were able to reveal this mystery.'" (Daniel 2:47 NIVASB)

Putting Daniel in charge of all the wise men in Babylon, King Nebuchadnezzar also made him ruler over the province of Babylon. Daniel's friends Shadrach, Meshach, and Abednego were appointed as administrators of Babylon, but Daniel remained at the royal court.

If you refer to the graphic image from the New International Version Study Bible, you can see the chart of Nebuchadnezzar's dream and Daniel's interpretation of it.

Most scholars believe the dream referred to four world empires, three of which would come after Nebuchadnezzar's Babylonian Empire. The second of those empires was the Medo-Persian Empire with which the Old Testament books Daniel, Haggai, Zechariah, Ezra, Nehemiah, Malachi, and Esther are concerned. We will be considering these Bible figures and their connection with the Persian Empire in further detail throughout *Rebuilding the Temple at Jerusalem.*

The third world empire covered in Nebuchadnezzar's dream was ruled by Alexander the Great and the Greeks. Daniel's vision of chapter 11 deals with Alexander as a powerful king; he does what he pleases, but as soon as he is established, his kingdom is broken up and given to others who are not his descendants. Alexander died after reigning only thirteen years, and since Alexander had no descendants, four of his generals divided up his kingdom.

If you are a Bible scholar, you will find reading Daniel's vision of chapter 11:5–45 with footnotes from the NIV Archaeological Study Bible will give you a tour of the dynasties established by two of Alexander's generals, Ptolemy and Seleucid. Immediately after Alexander's death in 323 BCE, Ptolemy "headed to Egypt and seized control of the administration, assuming the title of king in 305."[1] At that point Ptolemy became the king of the south of Daniel's vision.

Seleucid is the king of the north—as Daniel's vision tells us—who becomes even stronger than the king of the south. He originally rules Babylon but Ptolemy and Seleucid continue

---

1   *NIVASB*, "The Ptolemies" 1399

to battle for dominance, so the areas they rule do not always remain the same. As you study Daniel's vision of chapter 11, with footnotes, add the articles on Ptolemy, Seleucid,[2] and Antiochus IV Epiphanes in the NIV Archaeological Study Bible. These articles will help you understand Daniel's vision.

When the Greek Empire began to decline as the Romans steadily advanced into Greek territory, Antiochus IV Epiphanes [3] was the notorious ruler of the declining Seleucid arm of Alexander's empire, which included Judah among other nations.

As the fourth empire of Daniel's vision, the Romans advanced toward Jerusalem, and Antiochus, a vassal king of the declining Greek Empire, schemed to keep his crown as a vassal king under the Roman Empire. Uniting the various religions of nations in his territory under the god Zeus was the method Antiochus decided to use to impress Rome. The Jews were definitely not compliant where their religion was concerned, and the story of Antiochus's cruelty to the Jews will be told through the Apocrypha in chapter 10 of this book.

The fifth kingdom of Nebuchadnezzar's dream was interpreted in Daniel 2:44-45 as an everlasting kingdom of the God of Israel, which would never be destroyed or left to others. This kingdom would endure forever.

Discussion Questions

Look at Daniel 2:29–35 now, and compare it to the graphic of the statue on page 1301 of the NIV Study Bible and available in this chapter for your use.

---

[2] NIVASB, "The Seleucids," 1408.
[3] NIVASB, "Antiochus IV Epiphanes," 1406.

1. What empire is suggested by the head of pure gold? (See Graphic "Visions in Daniel" in this chapter.)
2. The chest of silver? (See Graphic "Visions in Daniel" in this chapter.)
3. The belly and thighs of bronze? (See Graphic "Visions in Daniel" in this chapter)
4. The legs, feet, and toes of iron and clay mixed together?
5. What might a lion indicate about the type of ruler Nebuchadnezzar was? (Your opinion, please)
6. How about the Persian Empire? What kind of empire would you expect when a bear symbolizes its authority? The symbol of Russia is a bear too. What kind of rule do you think that represents? (Your opinion)
7. What does Daniel's interpretation say about the fifth kingdom in Nebuchadnezzar's dream? (Daniel 2:44–45)
8. How long will it last? (See Daniel 2:44-45)
9. Who will conquer it? (See Daniel 2:44-45)
10. What kind of power, do you think, would be able to break iron, bronze, clay, silver, and gold to pieces?

Lecture 2

The Image of Gold and the Fiery Furnace

In the previous lecture, we mentioned that Daniel told King Nebuchadnezzar what his troubling dream was and interpreted it for him. The king's dream included an image with a head of gold and other body parts made of silver, bronze, and iron mixed with clay. A graphic of this image is included. If you will refer to this graphic in the previous chapter, it will help us understand events that followed the interpretation of Nebuchadnezzar's dream.

Influenced by Daniel's interpretation of Nebuchadnezzar's dream indicating that he is the king of kings or the head of gold of the image, in Daniel 3:7–12 we find King Nebuchadnezzar has built an image of gold ninety feet high and nine feet wide, setting it up in the province of Babylon.

Large statues of this kind were not made of solid gold but were plated with gold. It is suggested this statue probably represented the god Nabu, whose name formed the first part of Nebuchadnezzar's name (Nabu-kudurri-user, meaning Nabu, protect my son; (footnote to Daniel 3:1–2 NIVASB).

At the dedication, the king's herald stood in front of the statue and announced that people from every nation and language were commanded to fall down and worship the image of gold at the first sound of music played by horns, flutes, zithers, lyres, harps, and pipes. If they did not obey the command of the king, they would be immediately thrown into a blazing furnace.

Discussion Question

1. What do you think this huge image might represent to the people of Babylon?

You can find this story which is summarized below in Daniel 3.

Some of the wise men reported to the king that Shadrach, Meshach, and Abednego—Daniel's friends whom the king had put in charge of the affairs of the province of Babylon—had not obeyed the king's command. They ignored the king's commands to worship the image he had set up and refused to serve his god. Nebuchadnezzar was furious.

Just a note about the names of the musical instruments—*zither*, *harp*, and *pipe* are words Greek musicians used for musical instruments that were noted in Assyrian inscriptions before the time of Nebuchadnezzar (Footnote Dan.3:5). Poets and musicians were much prized in the ancient world, so these Greek words were introduced into popular use early in time by famed artists.

One of the arguments against Daniel as the author of the book traditionally considered to be written by him is the use of the Greek words for the musical instruments mentioned in Daniel 3:5. The use of these Greek words caused Daniel's authorship in the sixth century BC to be questioned. Greek didn't become the lingua franca until the Greek Empire came to power, so the use of Greek words before that time was questioned. Popular usage "of Greek words," in the case of musical instruments may have spread the names of the instruments through the Middle East.

Some scholars suggest the writing of Daniel during the time of the Maccabees would be more likely since the world was more Greek so words in Greek for musical instruments would naturally be included. In that case, however, one would expect more Greek words to be contained in the book of Daniel (see NIVASB article, "When Was Daniel Written? 1385).

We continue our paraphrase of the story found in Daniel 3:13–30. Nebuchadnezzar sent for Shadrach, Meshach, and Abednego. When they arrived, he asked them if it was true that they did not serve his gods or worship the golden image. Before they answered, he told them clearly what the herald had announced at the dedication in case they had not heard. You must fall down and worship the golden image the minute you hear the sound of music. If you don't obey, the fiery furnace is waiting for you. You won't find a god who can save you then.

Shadrach, Meshach, and Abednego were ready with their answer. They said, "Our God is able to save us from the fiery furnace but even if he does not, we will not serve your gods or worship the image you have built."

At their reply, Nebuchadnezzar became enraged. Fiercely he ordered the furnace heated seven times hotter for Shadrach, Meshach, and Abednego. He commanded his hardiest soldiers to tie the three of them up and throw them into the fire. The flames were so hot, the soldiers who threw them into the fire fell over dead.

When the king checked, he saw four men walking around in the fire. Shadrach, Meshach, and Abednego's robes, trousers, and turbans were untouched. Only the ropes that had bound them were destroyed.

The king, scarcely able to speak, said, "I thought there were only three men we threw into the fire. There is four of them now, completely unhurt and one of them looks like a son of the gods."

He shouted, "Shadrach, Meshach and Abednego, worshipers of the Most High God, come out!"

When they came out, nothing was touched by the fire—not one hair of their heads, their clothes, or their bodies.

King Nebuchadnezzar said, "Praise the God of Shadrach, Meshach and Abednego who has saved his servants! They were ready to die rather than worship any god except their own God. Therefore I command that the people of every nation who disrespect the God of Shadrach, Meshach and Abednego be cut into pieces and their houses be turned into piles of rubble, for no other god can save in this way."

Shadrach, Meshach, and Abednego got a promotion in the province of Babylon, where they served King Nebuchadnezzar.

Nebuchadnezzar was a historical figure who ordered many construction projects where he used bricks fired in kilns approaching 1,000 degrees centigrade. It is possible the furnace mentioned in our reading was one of those kilns. Archaeologists and Bible scholars have discovered that punishment by burning was well established in the ancient Near East (see Leviticus 21:9, 20:14; Genesis 38:24; Jeremiah 29:21–22).

The story of the furnace is pretty unbelievable until you remember the sages of India who walk across hot coals and lie on beds of nails.

We had a small communication company in Boulder, Colorado. When we lived in the Denver-Boulder area, a press release in *The Denver Post* announced that the Naropa Institute, an East Indian school for psychological studies in Boulder, was conducting a Saturday seminar for people who were interested in walking on hot coals.

They registered one hundred uninitiated people for their seminar, led by an East Indian guru, to experience the religious rite of walking on hot coals. A news report later said that all but one completely uninitiated person walked on the hot coals before the end of the Saturday seminar at 5:00 p.m.

Discussion Question

1. Can you think of some possible explanations for this type of phenomenon?

LECTURE 3

Nebuchadnezzar's Strange Malady

Daniel's interpretation of another of King Nebuchadnezzar's dreams can be followed in Daniel[4] in any version of the Bible:

King Nebuchadnezzar had a dream which terrified him. He sent for all the wise men of Babylon but as he asked each of them, none could interpret it for him. Finally Belteshazzar, chief of the magicians appeared before him. [Daniel's Babylonian name, Belteshazzar, was formed from Bel ("lord"), a title for the Babylonian god Marduk; footnote: Daniel 4:8 NIVASB].

King Nebuchadnezzar told him, "I know you have the spirit of the holy gods and can reveal all mysteries and can interpret the visions which passed before me while I was lying in my bed so listen to my dream."

In the middle of the land stood an enormous tree so tall, its branches touched the sky. The whole earth could see this tree, it was so huge and strong. Filled with beautiful leaves and weighed down with fruit, it fed all the creatures of the earth so there was food for all. The branches made homes for all the birds and sheltered all the beasts of the field.

---

4   Hicks, *A Soaring Spirit*, 16.

A holy messenger came down from heaven and called out in a loud voice, "Cut down the tree, trim off the branches, tear off the leaves and scatter the fruit. Let the birds and animals flee from its destruction.

Don't remove the stump and roots from the ground. There kept in place with an iron ring, let the man be drenched with the dew of heaven and live with the animals eating his fill of the grass in the pasture. Instead of the mind of a man, let his mind be changed into the mind of an animal, till seven times pass for him.

So that the living know that the Most High is over the kingdom of men and gives it to whomever he wishes and sets over them the lowliest of men.

King Nebuchadnezzar said, "That was my dream. You can tell me what it means Belteshazzar for you have the spirit of the holy gods in you. No other wise man could interpret it."

Then Daniel who was called Belteshazzar was speechless for a time because his thoughts alarmed him. The king quickly reassured him causing Belteshazzar to reply; "My Lord, if only the dream and its meaning applied to those who are against you! The tree you saw, immense and strong with its branches touching the sky, visible to all the earth, covered with leaves and abundant fruit for all, with nesting for birds and shelter for animals—you, O king, are that tree! You have become so great that your power reaches the ends of the earth. You saw a holy messenger coming down from heaven saying, "cut down the tree and destroy it but leave the stump and the roots in the ground held in place with an iron ring. Let him be drenched with dew of heaven and eat grass with the beasts of the field. Let him live like the wild animals until seven times pass."

"This is the interpretation—a decree from the Most High affects my lord the king: You will be driven away from people into the pasture to live with the wild animals. Your food will be grass and you will be washed with the dew of heaven. Seven times will pass by until you understand that the Most High rules over the kingdoms of men and gives them to anyone he wishes. Leaving the stump of the tree with its roots in place tells you your kingdom will be restored when you acknowledge that Heaven rules over all. Therefore O king, turn your back on your sin and do good. Be generous to the oppressed. Your peace of mind may be extended by such deeds." Our paraphrase of the narration of Nebuchadnezzar's dream ends in Dan. 4:27 of the New English Bible.

Nebuchadnezzar was reported to be an ambitious builder who was very proud of his projects. An important Old Testament idea is that "Pride goes before destruction and a haughty spirit before a fall" (Proverbs 16:18 NIV). It is often suggested in great literature that hubris is a fatal human flaw. Inordinate pride is associated with mental illness.

Motivation, energy, and drive are all believed to be gifts of God, and great accomplishments are not possible without those gifts. In addition to the gifts of God, many people are responsible for our success in life—our parents, teachers, and other mentors, as well as the craftspeople who work with us on various projects. To take total credit for our accomplishments is not accurate.

The Greek historian Megasthenes reported that "Nebuchadnezzar having ascended to the roof of his palace, became inspired by some god. (In antiquity insanity was looked upon as possession by a deity.)" (See Nebuchadnezzar's madness, NIVASB Article, 1391) That article calls Nebuchadnezzar's malady a delusional disorder called boanthropy, or cow-like behavior. Patients with similar disorders are reported to imagine themselves to be wolves.

"At the end of twelve months the king was walking on the roof of the royal palace at Babylon, and he exclaimed, "Is not this the great Babylon I have built as the royal residence, by my mighty power and for the glory of my majesty?"

The words were still on his lips, when a voice came down from heaven: 'To you, King Nebuchadnezzar, the word is spoken: the kingdom has passed from you. You are banished from the society of men and you shall live with the wild beasts; you shall feed on grass like oxen, and seven times will pass over you until you have learnt that the Most High is sovereign over the kingdom of men and gives it to whom he will.' At that very moment this judgment came upon Nebuchadnezzar. He was banished from the society of men and ate grass like oxen; his body was drenched by the dew of heaven, until his hair grew long like goats' hair and his nails like eagles' talons. (Daniel 4:29-33, NEB).

Discussion Question

1. What do you think might be happening to Nebuchadnezzar? Have you ever heard about a malady of this kind? Any ideas? (Your opinion)

At the end of the appointed time, I, Nebuchadnezzar, raised my eyes to heaven and I returned to my right mind. I blessed the Most High, praising and glorifying the Ever-living One.

At that very time I returned to my right mind and my majesty and royal splendor were restored to me for the glory of my kingdom. Now I, Nebuchadnezzar, praise and exalt and glorify the King of heaven; for all his acts are right and his ways are just and those whose conduct is arrogant he can bring low. (Daniel 4:34a, 36a, 37 NEB)

Discussion Questions

1. What do you think, now that you have heard the end of the story, which the Bible reports as the words of King Nebuchadnezzar himself? (Your opinion)

2. Does it seem possible to you that this is a real story, or do you think of it as a doubtful tale? Why or why not? (Your opinion)

3. If you think it is a real tale, now that you have heard the whole story, have you changed your mind about the cause of Nebuchadnezzar's malady? (Your opinion)

The last king of the Babylonian Empire was Nabonidus from Haran, the son of Nebuchadnezzar. His real interest was not serving the people. He was interested in old temples in his kingdom and so is sometimes referred to as the first archaeologist.

While Nabonidus was on a military expedition in the Arabian Peninsula, 4 Belshazzar, Nabonidus's son (Nebuchadnezzar's grandson) ruled during his father's absence, but he apparently wasn't any more interested in the people than his father was.

Some of you have heard of the city of Haran, Nabonidus's birthplace, through an earlier Bible story of Abraham. After Abraham and his father left the city of Ur, Terah, who was a worshipper of the moon god in Ur, stopped in Haran, where there were other moon worshippers. They settled in Haran until the death of Terah, when Abraham received instructions from his God to move on to the land of Canaan.

Over two thousand years later, King Nabonidus's mother was believed to have served as a priestess of the moon god, Sin, in that same city of Haran. Nabonidus apparently retained his loyalty to the god Sin from that relationship. Nabonidus left his son Belshazzar in control of Babylon under the Babylonian Empire while he remained in the Arabian Peninsula for ten years, during which time he apparently restored temples of various deities.

Discussion Questions

1. Does hearing the name of the moon god, Sin, make you wonder about the origin of the word *sin* in the Jewish religion?

2. What does the first commandment say about other gods? (If the first commandment, "You shall have no other Gods before me" (Exodus 20:3 NIV), is the most important one, then worship of "Sin," or the moon, might have been generalized into the use of *sin* as the word for disobedience of the commandments. What do you think?)

Conflict with the priests of the Babylonian god Marduk may have been an important ingredient of Nabonidus's lack of interest in palace affairs. Kings generally had an important role in the worship of the gods of the land. If Nabonidus's loyalty was to the moon god, Sin, he wouldn't have been very interested in fulfilling his religious duties to the god Marduk. Belshazzar, acting as regent in the place of his father, did not appear to be any more interested in ruling Babylon than his father was, judging from the commentary below from Daniel[5]. You can follow in any version of the Bible.

Belshazzar, the ruler gave a big party with one thousand of his nobles, his wives and his concubines celebrating there. He ordered the servants to bring in the gold and silver ceremonial cups for his guests' wine. Nebuchadnezzar plundered these gold and silver goblets from the temple when he conquered Jerusalem.

---

5 Isbouts, *The Biblical World*, 235, 238.

Placing them in the temple of Marduk indicated that Judah's God was in subjection to Marduk.

Drinking their wine and praising gods of gold, silver, bronze, iron, wood and stone, all of a sudden, the fingers of a human hand began writing on the wall, near the lampstand in the palace. Catching sight of the writing, the king's face turned white, his knees knocked and his legs buckled when he tried to stand.

Urgently calling for enchanters, astrologers and diviners to come at once, he announced that anyone who read the writing and told the king what it meant would be made the third highest ruler in the land.

Nabonidus was the first ruler and Belshazzar the second so the interpreter of the writing would be the third ruler after the royal family. All the wise men came in but they could not read the writing on the wall.

The king grew more agitated. The queen seated next to the king said, "Nebuchadnezzar appointed as chief of the wise men a man called Daniel who has the spirit of the holy gods in him."

Daniel was brought in and offered the position of the third highest ruler if he could read the writing. Daniel said, "You may keep your gifts for yourself but I will read the writing and tell its meaning to you. The Most High God gave King Nebuchadnezzar his kingdom with much greatness, glory and splendor. But when his heart became hardened with pride, his glory was taken from him. His heart was the heart of a beast so he was driven away from people and given the mind of an animal. He lived with donkeys and ate grass like cattle and his body was washed with the dew of heaven until he finally understood the Most High reigns over the kingdom of men and sets over them anyone he wishes. But you, O Belshazzar, have not humbled yourself though you knew this. You did not honor the God who holds your life in his hand. Therefore he sent the handwriting on the wall."

Discussion Question

1. Daniel served in the palace at Babylon and observed the behavior of the rulers. What do you think Daniel is implying?

The handwriting on the wall had the following words, which Daniel interpreted for the king: Mene, Mene, Tekel, Parsin (Daniel 5:25b). Isbouts says the words are Aramaic and would have appeared as mn, 'tql, prs.5

Possible interpretations of the writing might be as follows. Mina, shekel, and half mina/half shekel are weights—they may symbolize weighing the three rulers, Nebuchadnezzar, Nabonidus, and Belshazzar in a balance to discover their value as rulers. *Mene* may also represent weighing or *a Mina* as a unit of money. *Tekel* can also indicate weighed or weighing or suggest the weight of a shekel, possibly serving as a unit of money. *Peres* (singular of *Pursin*) can mean divided, or it can refer to Persia. A half mina or a half shekel may be weighing or a coin. (For further explanation, see the footnote at Daniel 5:26–28 NIVSB.)

Daniel was made the third highest ruler in the kingdom. "That very night Belshazaar king of the Chaldaeans was slain, and Darius the Mede took the kingdom" (Daniel 5:30, 31a NEB).

The palace at Babylon was taken by the Persian Empire on October 13, 539 BCE. At that time Cyrus the Persian was detained in a battle at the city of Opis. The governor of Babylon was battling Cyrus when he realized Persia was winning. He switched to the Persian side during battle. Cyrus sent him with troops to take the palace at Babylon for Persia. The governor of Babylon's name was Gobryas.

Possibly Gobryas was given the common Persian name Darius, or possibly someone else was put in charge whose name was Darius the Mede. Anyway, sixteen days later, Cyrus the Great marched through the wide-open Ishtar Gate, which was lined with cheering Babylonians throwing flowers. The city of Babylon gave in without a fight. Using the title king of Babylonia, Cyrus claimed he was selected to rule Babylon by the Babylonian god Marduk. Worshiping every day at Marduk's temple, he gained the approval of priests and the people.[6]

Discussion Questions

1. Do you think Cyrus the Persian worshiped the Babylonian god Marduk as a strategy to gain favor with the people?
2. What do you think of Cyrus the Persian's claim that the Babylonian god Marduk selected him to replace the Babylonian rulers?

---

6   Hicks, *A Soaring Spirit*, 9-39.

LECTURE 4

The Persian World Empire

The history of the Persian Empire is interesting because it fits right into today's news, which often includes the country of Iran, which is ancient Persia.

Aryan tribes who were ancestors of the Persians began to migrate to the area of Iran around 2000 BCE. Scholars believe these tribes made their way down the treeless steppes or plains of southern Russia. The most likely route is thought to have been through Turkestan, continuing down below the Caspian Sea to the Zagros Mountains, where their Aryan relatives, the Medes, settled earlier on the northwestern Iranian plateau.

Discussion Question

1. Where have we heard the name Aryan before? What notorious leader made a big deal about the Aryan race, calling Aryans the superior race?

Persians are descended from Aryan tribes around Russia. The dictionary says the Nazis thought of the Aryans as being of Nordic descent. Scandinavia is a neighbor of Russia. At any rate, these tribes migrated south until they came to the mountainous edge of the Iranian plateau. They settled there and called the area

Parsa. They lived for centuries in peace until Assyrian siege towers conquered Elam and its capital, Susa.[7]

Persia's cousins were the Medes. During the Persian period, King Cyaxares ruled the Medes. He allied his people with Babylon in 615 BCE, destroying Nineveh, the capital of Assyria. Media and Babylon split the Assyrian Empire between them. Babylon took southern Mesopotamia, Syria, and Palestine. The Medes got most of the rest. That is the reason the empire was known as the Medo-Persian Empire instead of the Persian Empire.

King Cyaxares's son Astyages assumed the throne of the Medes and arranged a marriage between his daughter Mandane and the ruler of Persia's ruling dynasty. Astyages had a troubling dream which the priests told him meant that Mandane's son was destined to conquer Media and all the lands beyond. Astyages ordered his chief steward to kill the newborn child, but instead the steward gave the child to a herdsman to raise.

When Astyages found out he had been tricked, he ordered the steward's own son to be killed and served to his father for dinner. The last course was the head of the steward's son. Nevertheless, whether his grandfather Astyages liked it or not, Mandane's child survived and became the ruler of the Persian Empire. He became known by the Greek form of his name, Cyrus the Persian.

In 559 BCE, Cyrus unified the Persians, rebuilding Susa to serve as his administrative capital. Meanwhile, Cyrus's grandfather Astyages became more oppressive, motivating silent opposition against him among his people, the Medes. Eventually, Astyages led the Medes against Cyrus, but Cyrus's troops seized Astyages, taking him in chains to Cyrus.

---

7   Hicks, *A Soaring Spirit*, 10.

Discussion Questions

1. Why do you think Astyages was attacking his own grandson?
2. Do you think the dream Astyages had before Cyrus was born had anything to do with his attack on Cyrus?

Instead of executing the man who tried to have him killed in infancy, Cyrus stripped him of his rank and title but allowed him to live. Then he marched to the city of Ecbatana to take over the Medes but left Median officials in their government posts. This strategy became the official trademark of Cyrus the Great as he occupied each new city.[8]

Cyrus the Great ruled Babylon from 539 until he was killed in battle in 530 BCE. Cyrus was an enlightened king. His empire controlled nearly two million square miles and ten million subjects. Revenue from nations sending various types of tribute equaled a million pounds of silver every year.

To control varied subjects in such a huge domain, Persia developed methods of governing that were extremely enlightened. Leaving local government and business staffs intact, Cyrus demanded only that subjects swear allegiance to the Persian Empire and pledge their payment of tribute. Citizens were free to live their own lives as long as they paid their taxes and did not impede the operation of the empire. Such methods gave Cyrus a reputation for being benevolent.

Local citizens, formerly dependents of Babylon, were eager to proclaim loyalty to the charitable Cyrus the Persian. Even the kings of Phoenicia pledged their first-class navy warships and strategic coastal cities to Cyrus's war machine.

---

8   Hicks, *A Soaring Spirit*, 9–23.

But Cyrus didn't just gather tribute from his subjects. The empire also improved the lives of Persian subjects as he expanded his war machine. For example, the Persians built an efficient road system so their army could cover long distances fast. Good, safe roads for ordinary citizens to travel as well as safe routes for camel caravans were a benefit to all conquered peoples.[9]

The Jewish prophet Isaiah began his prophetic career in the year 740 BCE. He prophesied concerning Cyrus nearly two hundred years before Cyrus began his reign of Babylon in 539 BCE. Isaiah prophesied,

I am the Lord ... who says of Cyrus, "He is my shepherd and will accomplish all that I please; he will say of Jerusalem, 'Let it be rebuilt,' and of the temple, 'Let its foundations be laid.'"

This is what the Lord says to his anointed, to Cyrus, whose right hand I take hold of to subdue nations before him and to strip kings of their armor, to open doors before him so that gates will not be shut: (Isaiah 44:24a, 28, 45:1 NIV)

Isaiah continued his ministry to Israel's kings from 740 BCE until some unknown time, when tradition reports he was sawn in two by King Manasseh because of his unfavorable prophecies against the king's idol worship. Manasseh is well known for offering his own son as a burnt offering at the places of idol worship that he restored after his father, King Hezekiah, tore them down. Manasseh ruled until 642 BCE.

During Isaiah's lifetime, he predicted Judah would fall to the Babylonian Empire because Israel followed Manasseh's example of idol worship. Daniel and the first group of royal exiles were taken to Babylon in 605 BCE, before Nebuchadnezzar destroyed Jerusalem. Isaiah also foretold the rise of the Persian Empire and the release of the Jewish exiles from Babylonian captivity by

---

9   Hicks, *A Soaring Spirit*, 17, 20.

Cyrus. Cyrus conquered Babylon in 539 BCE, but Isaiah did not live to see either of his prophecies fulfilled.

Jean-Pierre Isbouts's *Biblical World* names chapters 40–66 of Isaiah "Second Isaiah." That is a bow to the disagreement between scholars about the authorship of the latter part of the book of Isaiah. Isbouts feels there definitely was a different author of the second part of Isaiah. Many scholars, however, believe Isaiah could project his prophecy into the future to such an extent that his tone changed as he assured Israel, God would deliver them from the Babylonian captivity that he had foretold.

At any rate, Isaiah lived at least until 681 BC and is considered by most Bible scholars to have written chapters 40–66 during his later years. The second part of Isaiah is a type of apocalyptic writing that does project itself into the future in much the same way John projected his Revelation into the future.

The real issue about the author of Isaiah is that Jewish scribes editing ancient texts of Jewish writings in Babylon during the Persian period began to have a new vision of personal responsibility as well as of heaven and hell. The influence of the enlightened rule of Cyrus the Persian—and later Persian kings—appears to have given Israel a new vision of the monarchy. It is possible that new vision caused a different writer than Isaiah to pen the last chapters of Isaiah. It is also possible that Isaiah accepted this new vision of personal responsibility and wrote the last part of the chapter with a new attitude.

Cyrus the Persian proclaimed that any Jew who had been exiled to Babylon during the rule of the Babylonian Empire could return to Judah and rebuild the walls of Jerusalem and the temple. That was an enlightened act for a powerful dictator king.

Discussion Questions

1. From what you already have heard of Cyrus, do you think he might have been an enlightened benevolent ruler? Why do you think that? (Your opinion)

2. Do you think his methods might have been motivated by considerations other than benevolence? Explain your answer. (Your opinion)

Religion of the Medes and Persians

We may well question why Cyrus's policies were so enlightened for that time period in history. First of all, Cyrus's father was a ruler of the Persian dynasty, and Persia was an ancient and advanced civilization. Very likely the religion of the neighboring Medes also had a bearing on Cyrus's behavior. Beginning twelve hundred years before the birth of Christ and continuing for six hundred years in the kingdom of the Medes, the influence of the prophet Zarathustra transformed the Persian faith. Zoroaster was the Greek form of the name Zarathustra.

All the Persian kings who followed Darius I "conquered in the name of a supreme being, Ahura Mazda the Wise Lord, creator of heaven and earth"[10] who appeared to Zoroaster in a vision revealing himself as the only supreme deity creator, all seeing and all powerful representative of light and truth.

Previously, Persian deities were nature gods with little individual significance. Zoroaster's vision of Ahura Mazda as the creator and the powerful representative of light and truth caused him to promote Ahura Mazda as the supreme god of Persia.

---

10   Hicks, A Soaring Spirit, 37

Zoroaster pictured the universe in a constant battle between good and evil, with light and truth emerging triumphant. The blessed of Ahura Mazda would find salvation in heaven, while all others would roast in a fiery purgatory.

The Persian concept of one god, or monotheism, was not new to the Middle East. The Egyptian Pharaoh Akhenaten in 1400 BCE introduced the idea of one god to Egypt, but his son Tutankhamun, influenced by his dissatisfied subjects, reverted back to the old gods when he became king. Leaders of the Jews also taught worship of one God for centuries, following the lead of Abraham.

Zoroaster, however, gave monotheism a new twist. His viewpoint of a moral struggle between forces of light and darkness appeared to promote praiseworthy behavior in Cyrus the Great, as well as in other rulers of the Persian Empire.[11]

Discussion Questions

1. Does the concept of a constant battle between good and evil remind you of our own Western ideas of good and evil? (Opinion)
2. Does the Hebrew creation story of the snake tempter include elements of a struggle between good and evil also?
3. Do you think the Persian Empire's religious beliefs influenced the Jews during their 228 years of power? (Your opinion. Explain your answer.)

At Cyrus's death, his son Cambyses reigned. Under his father, he had been the able Persian governor of Babylonia. Now he

---

11 Hicks, *A Soaring Spirit*, 37-38

intended to prove himself in battle. He attacked Egypt, whose leaders had regained much of the lost prestige of their old kingdom. At this point, though, the Pharaoh Ahmose was an old man, and as Persian troops approached, he died. At the Battle of Pelusium in 525 BCE the Persians, under Cambyses, added Egypt to their empire.

Cambyses tried to conduct himself in the enlightened tradition of his father, but when he took the title of Egyptian pharaoh, he was assuming the cultural title of deity, commanding total devotion from all his subjects. Egyptians even married their own family members to keep the god and goddess line pure. Under this stress, Cambyses began to stumble.

Bad decisions began to plague him. A decision to attack Carthage nearly fostered mutiny among his Phoenician navy because Cambyses ignored the fact that the people of Carthage were relatives of the Phoenicians. On one war expedition, Cambyses's provisions ran out, causing the troops to eat their own pack animals. Reports of cannibalism among the troops caused Cambyses to retreat.

Reportedly, Cambyses grew more proud and despotic, acting as if he were completely out of his mind. At one point, in a frenzy of rage, he kicked his pregnant wife, who was also his sister, to death. He eventually died of a wound that reportedly was self-inflicted. He ruled for eight years (530–522 BCE).[12]

Discussion Question

Cambyses made an effort to be the kind of enlightened ruler that Cyrus had been, but he was unable to manage it.

1. Why do you think he could not manage the enlightened rule that Cyrus introduced?

---

12 Hicks, *A Soaring Spirit*, 22–23.

LECTURE 5

Cyrus the Great Decrees that Jewish Exiles May Return to Jerusalem to Rebuild the Temple

Apparently Cyrus the Persian actually believed that the gods selected him to be the king of kings. When he conquered a new nation, he publicly recognized their gods, announcing that the national gods had summoned him to rule their nation. He made traditional offerings to the gods of each nation. This practice did not appear to be simply a technique to make ruling the Persian Empire easier. Cyrus appeared to actually believe he was commissioned to rule in this manner.

Discussion Questions

1. How do you think our current heads of state relate to the gods of other nations, if at all? United States official policy on holy places such as temples and churches during war?

As was mentioned in lecture 4, the prophet Isaiah foretold the destruction of the temple and mentioned the name of Cyrus as one who would initiate the rebuilding of the temple (Isaiah 44:28

NIV) before Jerusalem was destroyed and long before Cyrus was born.

Jeremiah prophesied seventy years of Babylonian rule and captivity for the Jews (Jeremiah 25:11–12). The end of the seventy years of captivity was 538 BCE. Jerusalem and its temple still lay in ruins, with piles of rubble marking the borders of the city where the wall once stood. After approximately seventy years of Babylonian captivity, Cyrus the Persian conquered Babylon (539 BCE) and proclaimed freedom for Jewish captives who had been exiled to Babylon by Nebuchadnezzar. Jews wishing to return to Jerusalem to rebuild their temple were free to do so.

The Hebrew language record of Cyrus's proclamation is written in the first chapter of Ezra as follows:

Thus saith Cyrus King of Persia. The Lord God of heaven hath given me all the kingdoms of the earth; and he hath charged me to build him a house at Jerusalem, which is in Judah.

Who is there among you of all his people? His God be with him, and let him go up to Jerusalem, which is in Judah, and build the house of the Lord God of Israel, (he is the God,) which is in Jerusalem. (Ezra 1:2–4 KJV)

Discussion Questions

1. What do you think prophecy is? Divine providence? Astute observations by persons who have studied human nature? Hebrew numerology? Or something else?

2. What do you think of the prophecy of Jeremiah in regard to seventy years of Jewish captivity?

3. What do you think of Isaiah's prophecy in regard to Cyrus and the rebuilding of the temple two hundred years prior to the time of Cyrus?

Ezra reported that as a result of Cyrus's proclamation, the tribal families of Judah and Benjamin and the priestly clan of the Levites—in fact, everyone who felt moved to return to Jerusalem to rebuild the temple—prepared themselves. Neighbors gave them their treasures of silver and gold, household goods, livestock, other valuable gifts, and offerings.

King Cyrus added the silver and golden temple goblets and other temple vessels that Nebuchadnezzar had taken from the temple when he conquered Jerusalem. These temple vessels had been placed in the temple of Marduk to show that Marduk had dominated the God of the Jews. Mithredath the treasurer counted the temple vessels out to Sheshbazzar the prince of Judah.

"Sheshbazzar is a Babylonian name, but he was probably a Jewish official acting as a deputy governor of Judah under the Persian satrap in Samaria. It was common for Jews in Babylon to receive "official" Babylonian names(cf Da.1:7) and some scholars believe that Sheshbazzar and Zerubbabel were in fact the same person. Both were governors (Ezra 5:14; Haggai 1:1, 2:2), both are said to have laid the foundation of the temple (Ezra 3:2–8, 5:16; Haggai 1:14–15; Zechariah 4:6–10), and Josephus (Antiquities, 11.1.3) seems to have identified Sheshbazzar with Zerubbabel"(see footnote Ezra 1:8 NIVASB).

Sheshbazzar brought 5,400 articles of silver and gold from Babylon to Jerusalem, including the following:

Gold dishes	30
Silver dishes	1,000
Silver pans	29
Gold bowls	30
Matching silver bowls	410
Other articles	1,000

The inventory above is found in Ezra 1:9-11, New International Version.

Thousands of people of Judah responded to Cyrus's proclamation, inviting Jews to return from Babylonian captivity to their own town in Judah. Those electing to return (42,360) left in company with Zerubbabel and arrived in 538 BCE finding Jerusalem in ruins.

According to Ezra 2:68–70, when the exiles arrived at the ruined site of the house of the Lord in Jerusalem, some heads of families gave freewill offerings of gold and silver for the rebuilding of the house of God; plus they donated one hundred garments for the priests. Priests. Levites, singers, gatekeepers and temple servants, and others that were with them settled in their own towns.

After the returning exiles got settled, they all assembled in Jerusalem during the seventh month, a holy month of the Jewish calendar. Ezra reports in chapter 3:1–7 that Jeshua, son of Jozadak, and his fellow priests and Zerubbabel and his brothers began building the altar of the God of Israel in order to sacrifice burnt offerings to the Lord as written in the laws of Moses. The peoples around them were hostile, but they completed the altar and offered evening and morning burnt offerings even though they were afraid.

Money was donated for masons and carpenters, as well as food and drink and oil for the people of Sidon and Tyre. Cyrus, King of Persia, had already authorized logs from the cedars of Lebanon for rebuilding the temple, but the people furnished needed products and payments for workmen who would be bringing the logs.

Wood and stone were scarce in most of the Middle East, so cedar logs had been brought from Lebanon for building the original temple in the time of Solomon. Now, five hundred years later, Cyrus furnished cedar logs from Lebanon to rebuild the temple.

As the builders were laying the foundation, priests in their vestments, with trumpets, and the Levites, with cymbals, stood near to praise the Lord as King David of Israel had decreed five hundred years earlier. With praise and thanksgiving they sang to the Lord of his goodness and his steadfast love to Israel.

When the enemies of Judah and Benjamin heard that the exiles were building a temple for the Lord, the God of Israel, they came to Zerubbabel and to the heads of the families and said, "Let us build too because, like you, we seek your God and have been sacrificing to him since the time of Esarhaddon, king of Assyria, who brought us here."

But Zerubbabel, Jeshua, and the rest of the heads of the families of Israel answered, "You have no part with us in building a temple to our God. We alone will build it for the Lord, the God of Israel, as King Cyrus, the King of Persia, commanded us." (Ezra 4:1-2, NIVASB)

The Samaritans were one of several factions that continued to delay the rebuilding of Jerusalem after the Jewish exiles from Babylon returned to rebuild Jerusalem. The Jews and the Samaritans had been enemies for centuries. King David united all the twelve tribes of Israel, but after the death of King Solomon, only the tribes of Judah and Benjamin remained part of the House of David. The rest of the ten tribes of Israel rebelled against the new king, Rehoboam, when they asked for relief from heavy taxation. Rehoboam replied, "My father made your yoke heavy, and I will add to your yoke; my father also chastised you with whips, but I will chastise you with scorpions" (1 Kings 12:14 KJV).

From that day forward, ten of the twelve tribes separated themselves from the House of David, settling in the northern part of Israel under Jeroboam. Samaria was their major city, and they called themselves Samaritans.

Jeroboam, their leader, fearing that the ten tribes of Israel would return to offer sacrifices at the temple at Jerusalem, made two golden calves, placing one in Dan and one in Bethel. Jeroboam announced to them, "It is too much for you to go up to Jerusalem: behold thy gods, O Israel, which brought thee up out of the land of Egypt" (1 Kings 12:28 KJV).

The northern kingdom of Israel fell to Assyria in 721 BCE.[13] As is noted in Ezra 4:2, some Samaritans were exiled to the city of Jerusalem by Assyria's King Esarhaddon, so perhaps some of the exiled Samaritans did try to worship with the Jews in Jerusalem. This deportation of the Samaritans was more than 130 years before the fall of Jerusalem. During the centuries after Assyria deported the northern kingdom of Israel out of Samaria, those tribes became known as the ten lost tribes of Israel.

Discussion Questions

1. Why were the Samaritans living in Judah? (See Ezra. 4:2)
2. What caused the long-standing enmity between the Jews and the Samaritans? (See I Ki. 12:14-28)
3. How did the ten lost tribes of Israel get lost? See Ezra 4:2, also footnotes from Ezra 4:1-2 NIVASB
4. Do you think deportation to Jerusalem did encourage the Samaritans to worship the God of the Jews? (See Ezra 4:2 also footnotes from Ezra 4:1-2, NIVASB)

---

13 *Eerdmans*, Samaria

5. Do you think the Jews should have accepted the Samaritans' offer of help in rebuilding the temple at Jerusalem? (reader's opinion)

Then the groups who had been deported into Judah realized that the Jews intended to rebuild their country for their own use. Trying to protect the life they had made for themselves while the Jews from Judah were exiled in Babylon, they tried to make the Jews fear them in order to stop the rebuilding efforts. Trying to upset their plans, they hired laborers to work against them. This behavior continued from the reign of King Cyrus of Persia until the reign of King Darius of Persia.

Cyrus ruled Judah from 539–530 BCE, and Darius took the throne in 522 BCE. The Jews arrived in Judah from exile in 538 BCE, so rebuilding was opposed in Judah for at least fifteen years. Possibly the Jews with their background of occupation by foreign troops didn't believe they had the right to appeal to Cyrus, so the temple just didn't get finished in Cyrus's reign. The delay also included the eight years of Cambyses's reign (530–522 BCE) until Darius I replaced Cambyses in 522 BCE.

Lecture 6

Cambyses's Brief Reign Followed by Darius I

Daniel served the Babylonian and Persian Empires from 605 BCE to 537 BCE, about seventy years. He lived to see Cyrus the Persian proclaim freedom for Jewish exiles so they could leave Babylon to rebuild the temple in Jerusalem, and he actually saw the first group leave. Cyrus the Great ruled from 559–530 BCE. His son Cambyses took the throne in 530 and ruled until 522 BCE. He extended the empire into Egypt, Cyprus, and the Greek islands.

To review a previous lecture; Cambyses tried to follow the enlightened rule of his father. When he became pharaoh of Egypt, though, his rule began to show signs of difficulty. Egyptians worshiped their rulers as gods, even marrying their own family members to keep the lines of deity pure. Cambyses began to make bad decisions under this type of stress.

A decision to attack Carthage nearly caused mutiny among his Phoenician navy because Cambyses was not sensitive to the fact that the people of Carthage were relatives of the Phoenicians. Poor planning caused Cambyses's provisions to fail during a war expedition. Reports of cannibalism among the troops caused Cambyses to retreat.

Under the stress of leadership Cambyses reportedly became a despot. In a rage, he kicked his pregnant wife, who was also his sister, to death. He often appeared to be out of his mind. Eventually Gaumata—a member of the magi, or wise men—led a revolt, masquerading as Cambyses's younger brother. He was killed by Cambyses. The king died under mysterious circumstances, possibly of a wound reported to have been self-inflicted. He ruled for eight years (530–522 BCE).[14]

Darius I was a distant cousin of the Achaemenid satrap of Parthia. He executed Gaumata and proclaimed himself king; then he put down revolts for the next two years. By 518 he was the acknowledged ruler, even in distant territories of the empire. He ruled from 522 to 486 BCE.

The Persian realm under Darius was a sophisticated mix of Persian central government and local leadership. The administrative officers of the Persian Empire were appointed by Darius I and were called satraps. Most satraps were Persian aristocrats. They administered twenty large satrapies, which were regional units including more than one province.[15] Subordinates of the satraps were often local people who were well known in the community and thus were able to use local know-how to help Persians govern effectively. Above the satrap were officers called, "the eyes and ears of the king."

Darius I contributed more to the well-being of the realm than other Persian kings after Cyrus. He improved the 1,700-mile royal road from Sardis, through Mesopotamia, to the capital at Susa. Soldiers patrolled year-round to keep it safe. Laborers maintained it by hard-packing the earth; laying stones when necessary; and building ferry crossings, checkpoints, and inns that were a day's

---

14 Hicks, *A Soaring Spirit*, 22–23.
15 *NIVSB*, footnote to Esther 1:1.

travel apart. Other highways branched out from there to other centers throughout the empire.

Darius I's royal messenger service relayed official documents to fresh riders and horses every fifteen miles. Messengers were so reliable that a comment by Herodotus about the dependability of Persian messengers is echoed in the mission of the US Post Office: "Nothing stops these couriers from covering their allotted stage in the quickest possible time—neither snow, rain, heat, nor darkness."(Hicks, Soaring Spirit, 29)[16]

On the floodplain of the Nile, the Tigris, and the Euphrates Rivers were huge estates with crops of barley, millet, flax, wheat, and dates maintained by serfs. Landowners were usually Persian noblemen who gained their land for service rendered to the crown. The land was generally awarded for military service. High-ranking officials were awarded large acreages.

Darius sent engineers to Babylon to renew irrigation ditches in the floodplain to increase crop yields. Water for crops had to be transported to arid regions in the mountains and areas of the Iranian Plateau from mountain springs. It was sent through underground tunnels to keep it from evaporating in the desert. These tunnels were called qanats. Shafts dug from the surface at regular intervals into the underground aqueducts accommodated maintenance workers.

One of Darius I's best-known reforms was converting bartering of goods to a coin-operated economy. By limiting the minting of coins to royal minters and standardizing values on each gold daric, which bore the emperor's image, Darius created an economy in which coins were accepted without question. Weights and measures were also standardized by the king. Universal law; good,

---

16 Hicks, *A Soaring Spirit*, 23-32

safe roads; sound currency; and standard weights and measures enabled the whole empire to become a common market.

Papyrus came from Egypt; spices, gold, and gems from India; silver, copper, and iron from the mines of Anatolia; textiles from Carthage; purple dye from Phoenicia; carpets from Iran; and timber from Lebanon. The Egyptian Canal was completed under the Persians and linked the Indian Ocean, the Red Sea, the Nile, and the Mediterranean, making trade even more convenient. Voyages of exploration into the Aegean Sea and down Africa's west coast were also undertaken and supported by the emperor.[17]

Discussion Questions

1. From the information about Darius, what do you think the subjects of Darius thought of their king? (reader's opinion)
2. Compare Darius's irrigation projects, which sent water through underground tunnels, with the Colorado River project, which sends water to California through open canals. Which is more water efficient? (Underground tunnels keep water from evaporating in the desert.)
3. What do you think about Darius's standardization of coins? (reader's opinion)
4. Do you think our Western civilization benefited from the Persian Empire? (opinion please)

The first day of the Persian new year was the festival of the spring equinox. As many as ten thousand subjects from twenty nations made the journey to Persepolis, where Darius I built a ceremonial capital for Persian subjects to honor the king with their tribute.

---

17 Hicks, *A Soaring Spirit*, 23–32.

Bas reliefs from the massive center at Persepolis show Assyrians bringing bowls, possibly made of silver or gold, and ponies. A lion cub from Susa is shown, as are Cilicians bringing prize rams; Scythians offering a stallion; a Bactrian leading a camel; East Indians balancing double containers on their shoulders, perhaps filled with gold dust; and Ionians holding out balls of yarn to the king while Lydians presented ornate armbands.

Scribes kept records of royal transactions in several languages because of the variety of cultures under Persian control. However, records of gifts in the royal vaults at Persepolis and Susa were kept in Elamite, since most clerks knew that language. Rooms of gilt furniture, crystal, textiles, armor, and other objects were carefully catalogued on both parchment and clay tablets. Darius made Aramaic, a language of Syrian origin, the official language of the empire.[18] State business was conducted in that language. Jesus still spoke Aramaic even though the official language was Greek by that time.

The multilingual nature of the Persian Empire was reflected in the three languages generally displayed on monuments throughout the realm quoting the king's proclamations. These languages were Elamite; Akkadian, which was the Babylonian language; and Darius's childhood language, which was old Persian, a nomadic language with no written script for which Darius's scribes invented a written form. Inscriptions on monuments became the means for scholars to decipher Mesopotamia's writing system.[19]

King Darius I assisted with the rebuilding of the temple, which we will follow in the story we are using from the book of Haggai.

The prophet Haggai was born in exile in Babylon and returned to Jerusalem after the decree of Cyrus the Persian to rebuild the

---

18   Bertman, *Handbook to Life in Ancient Mesopotamia*, 83.
19   Hicks, *A Soaring Spirit*, 31–32. s

temple at Jerusalem. Zechariah, a contemporary of Haggai's, was also born in exile and returned to Jerusalem with the Jews who planned to rebuild. Zechariah's prophecies appear to have ministered directly to the people's religious and emotional needs rather than the physical rebuilding of the temple, but Haggai's prophecies were directed toward rebuilding the temple.

Even with Cyrus the Great's proclamation to rebuild the temple at Jerusalem, rebuilding was stymied by concentrated opposition from various exiles who were settled in the area by Assyria or Babylonian conquerors. After Cyrus's death, his son Cambyses was apparently unaware of his father's project to rebuild the temple. At any rate, he is not mentioned in the Bible in connection with efforts to rebuild the temple.

When King Darius came to power and efforts to unseat him were finally settled, the prophet Haggai began to agitate for rebuilding of the temple. In Haggai 1 (NJPS) we find the following account after the new king had reigned for two years. Haggai delivered this paraphrased message from the Lord to the people:

The people are saying, "It's not time yet for rebuilding the Temple." But they are dwelling in their paneled houses while the Temple lies in shambles. This is what I heard from the Lord. People, you have planted but not harvested much; you eat a lot but aren't satisfied; you drink but are still thirsty; you cover yourselves but you're still cold and when you earn some silver, it falls through holes in your purse. It's time to go up to the hills and get timber to rebuild the Temple so the Lord is pleased with you.

Zerubbabel and all the Jews dwelling in Judah obeyed the message that Haggai delivered to them because he was sent by the Lord and the people feared the Lord. They started the work on the house of the Lord, their God on the twenty fourth day of the sixth month in the second year of King Darius according to the Jewish calendar.

According to our calendar (footnote to Haggai 1:15 NIVASB), that date was September 21, 520 BCE.

About the time the Jews got a good start on the temple, their enemies began to come around to hassle them. Ezra 5 gives us an interesting description of the workers' experiences with the officials of the area. Tattenai, the governor of the province of Beyond the River, was first on the scene. From the perspective of the people living in Babylon, the region of Judah was definitely beyond the River Euphrates. It was also called Trans-Euphrates.

Tattenai asked the workmen, "Who gave you permission to rebuild this building and what is the name of the workers?" But the builders did not delay while a report from the officials went to Darius and they waited for the reply. They knew their God was watching over them so they kept working on the temple.

Discussion Questions

1. What do you think Haggai's reply may have been to Tattenai when he asked who authorized the reconstruction of the temple? (Your opinion)

2. Since King Cyrus had authorized the rebuilding of the temple eighteen years before, why do you suppose the Jews did not complain to King Cyrus when rebuilding efforts were thwarted by the enemies of the Jews? (Conquered peoples are not used to having rights.)

Judah's opponents complained when the Jews started to rebuild. This is a copy of the letter that Tattenai, governor of Trans-Euphrates ... sent to King Darius:

To King Darius, greetings and so forth. Be it known to the king, that we went to the province of Judah, to the house of the great God. It is being rebuilt of hewn stone, and wood is being laid in the walls. The work is being done with dispatch and is going well. Thereupon we directed this question to these elders, "Who issued orders to you to rebuild this house and to complete its furnishings?" We also asked their names so that we could write down the names of their leaders for your information. (Ezra 5:7b–10 NJPS)

Very likely Tattenai, the governor of Trans-Euphrates, was one of the settlers in the area appointed by the Persian Empire to govern the Trans-Euphrates district. He says to the Jews rebuilding the temple, "Who gave you permission to build here?"

Discussion Questions

1. Have you ever encountered this kind of response when you took the initiative on a project? (Your reply)
2. Why are people so quick to say, "Who gave you permission to do this?" (Your answer, please)

The letter to the king from the governor and his associates continues with the information that the Jews gave to Tattenai when they were questioned. The complete letter can be found in Ezra 5:3-17 but we will summarize it here.

Tattenai repeated the information supplied by the Jews. "They said they were servants of the God of heaven and earth who were rebuilding the temple built by a great king of Israel. But because the Jews disobeyed the God of heaven, he handed them over to Nebuchadnezzar the Chaldean, king of Babylon, who destroyed the temple and deported the people to Babylon."

Tattenai continued his account in Ezra 5:3-17 of the New JPS Translation, which is paraphrased below.

In the first year that King Cyrus reigned, he issued an edict to rebuild this House. He also released the silver and gold ceremonial vessels which Nebuchadnezzar had taken from the temple and placed in the temple of Babylon to one called Sheshbazzar whom he appointed governor. His instructions were for him to place these vessels in the temple at Jerusalem when the house of God is rebuilt in its original site. That same Sheshbazzar laid the foundation and worked on its reconstruction but the building is not yet finished.

If it please the king, please check the royal archives in Babylon for the order said to be issued by King Cyrus and let us know how to proceed in this matter. This concludes the narrative in Chapter 5:3-17, paraphrased above.

Ecbatana, Babylon, Persepolis, and Susa were the four capitals of the Persian Empire. King Darius then issued an order, and they searched in the archives stored in the treasury at Babylon. A scroll was found in the citadel of Ecbatana in the province of Media, and this was written on it:

Memorandum:

In the first year of King Cyrus, King Cyrus issued an order concerning the House of God in Jerusalem: "Let the house be rebuilt, a place for offering sacrifices, with a base built up high. Let it be sixty cubits high and sixty cubits wide, with a course of unused timber for each three courses of hewn stone. The expenses shall be paid by the palace. And the gold and silver vessels of the House of God which Nebuchadnezzar had taken away from the temple in Jerusalem and transported to Babylon shall be returned, and let each go back to the temple in Jerusalem where it belongs: you shall deposit it in the House of God.

"Now you, Tattenai, governor of the province of Beyond the River, Shethar-Bozenai and colleagues, the officials of the province of Beyond the River, stay away from that place. Allow the work of this House of God to go on; let the governor of the Jews and the elders of the Jews rebuild this House of God on its site.

And I hereby issue an order concerning what you must do to help these elders of the Jews rebuild this House of God: the expenses are to be paid to these men with dispatch out of the resources of the king, derived from the taxes of the province of Beyond the River, so that the work [will] not be stopped. They are to be given daily, without fail, whatever they need of young bulls, rams, or lambs as burnt offering for the God of Heaven … so that they may offer pleasing sacrifices to the God of Heaven and pray for the life of the king and his sons.

I also issue an order that whoever alters this decree shall have a beam removed from his house, and he shall be impaled on it and his house confiscated. And may the God who established His name there cause the downfall of any king or nation that undertakes to alter or damage that House of God in Jerusalem. I, Darius, have issued the decree, let it be carried out with dispatch." (Ezra 6:3–12 NJPS)

Because of the decree King Darius sent, Tattenai, governor of Trans-Euphrates, and Shethar-Bozenai and their associates were careful to assist the reconstruction efforts of the Jews. They finished the temple in the sixth year of the reign of King Darius.

"The restoration was completed on March 12, 516 B.C., almost 70 years after its destruction. The renewed work had begun on September 21, 520 B.C. (Haggai 1:15), and sustained effort had continued for about three and a half years" (footnote at Ezra 6:15 NIVASB). That was twenty-three years after Cyrus decreed that the temple be rebuilt.

Discussion Questions

1. Do you think Cyrus the Great would have allowed the local officials in Judah to circumvent the rebuilding of the temple if he had known about it? (Opinion please)
2. Why do you think Haggai didn't write Darius asking for permission to finish rebuilding efforts? (Your opinion, please)

Apparently King Darius I's interest in Judah did not extend beyond rebuilding the temple. There is no other mention of King Darius I in regard to the work of rebuilding the city of Jerusalem. At his death in 486 BCE, Egypt rebelled and Xerxes, the son of Darius, had to march west to suppress the revolt (footnote to Ezra 4:6 NIVSB).

Xerxes apparently did not take part in rebuilding Jerusalem. He ruled from 486 to 465 BCE.

Lecture 7

Xerxes's Only Connection to the Rebuilding of Jerusalem

The only place Xerxes is included in Hebrew scriptural writings in regard to Rebuilding the Temple at Jerusalem is the following verse in Ezra: "At the beginning of the reign of Xerxes they lodged an accusation against the people of Judah and Jerusalem" (Ezra 4:6 NIV).

They in this verse refers to those in Jerusalem who were opposed to the rebuilding of the city. That is the only mention of King Xerxes in connection with rebuilding efforts in Judah.

Darius I died in 486 BCE. Egypt took that opportunity to rebel against the Persian Empire. Xerxes, his son and the heir apparent, immediately took troops to Egypt to put down the rebellion. So at the beginning of Xerxes's reign, letters coming to him would probably have been handled by King Darius's grand vizier, if indeed they were handled at all.

Discussion Question

1. With the king dead and the new king off to Egypt to battle, what might have been the scenario at the palace? (Complete confusion)

The scenario at the palace would no doubt have been a palace staff in complete disorder after the death of their king and the immediate absence of the new king, Xerxes. Obviously there would have been great difficulty in handling mail to the dead king with no new king in charge in the palace. Bookkeeping and filing for the new king would have been imprecise, if not totally nonexistent, since officials for the new king probably would not have been appointed.

In addition to that, the account in Ezra 4:7 says the letter to Xerxes from the province of Judah was written in Aramaic, which had to be translated. Even Ezra's record of the letter to Xerxes is undated in the writings of Ezra. Such turmoil at the beginning of Xerxes's reign may have kept him from becoming aware of the rebuilding problems in the province of Judah. Whatever happened, we hear no more about Xerxes in regard to reconstruction of Jerusalem or other cities in the province of Judah.

At the death of Xerxes, twenty years later, he was replaced by his son Artaxerxes I, who was king from 465 to 425 BCE. Ezra was a scribe. We don't know how he managed to get the attention of Artaxerxes, but the record (Ezra 7:1b, 6–8) shows that he journeyed to Jerusalem with a letter from the king.

During the seventh year of the reign of Artaxerxes, king of Persia (458 BCE), Ezra arrived at Jerusalem from Babylon with a letter from the king. The Bible text tells us he was very familiar with the law of Moses. It also says that the king gave him everything he wanted because his God was with him. At the same time, some priests, Levites, singers, gatekeepers, and temple servants also came with him from Babylon.

This is a copy of the letter King Artaxerxes had given to Ezra the priest and teacher, a man learned in matters concerning the commands and decrees of the Lord of Israel:

Artaxerxes, King of Kings,

To Ezra, the priest a teacher of the Law of the God of heaven: Greetings.

Now I decree that any of the Israelites in my kingdom, including priests and Levites, who wish to go to Jerusalem with you, may go. You are sent by the king and his seven advisers to inquire about Judah and Jerusalem with regard to the Law of your God, which is in your hand. Moreover, you are to take with you the silver and gold that the king and his advisers have freely given to the God of Israel, whose dwelling is in Jerusalem, together with all the silver and gold you may obtain from the province of Babylon, as well as the free will offerings of the people and priests for the temple of their God in Jerusalem. With this money be sure to buy bulls, rams and male lambs, together with their grain offerings and drink offerings, and sacrifice them on the altar of the temple of your God in Jerusalem.

You and your brother Jews may then do whatever seems best with the rest of the silver and gold, in accordance with the will of your God. Deliver to the God of Jerusalem all the articles entrusted to you for worship in the temple of your God. And anything else needed for the temple of your God that you may have occasion to supply, you may provide from the royal treasury.

Now I, King Artaxerxes, order all the treasurers of Trans-Euphrates to provide with diligence whatever Ezra the priest, a teacher of the Law of the God of heaven, may ask of you—up to a hundred talents of silver, a hundred cors of wheat, a hundred baths of wine, a hundred baths of olive oil, and salt without limit. Whatever the God of heaven has prescribed, let it be done with diligence for the temple of the God of heaven. Why should there be wrath against the realm of the king and of his sons? You are also to know that you have no authority to impose taxes, tribute or duty on any of the priests, Levites, singers, gatekeepers, temple servants or other workers at this house of God.

Artaxerxes ends his letter with, And you, Ezra, in accordance with the wisdom of your God, which you possess, appoint magistrates and judges to administer justice to all the people of Trans-Euphrates—all who know the laws of your God. And you are to teach any who do not know them. Whoever does not obey the law of your God and the law of the king must surely be punished by death, banishment, confiscation of property, or imprisonment." (Ezra 7:11–26 NIVASB)

Discussion Questions

1. Why would a king of another religion want Ezra to offer sacrifices to his god for the king and his sons? (In the Cyrus Cylinder, Cyrus the Great proclaimed himself to be beloved of the gods Bel, Nebo, and Marduk, deities of Babylon. Darius would also be called the new "son of Ra."[20] Ra was an Egyptian King. In Ezra, Cyrus says, "The Lord, the God of heaven, has given me all the kingdoms of the earth" [Ezra 1:2].)

2. Have you heard the expression "placate the gods"? (Another possible reason for Artaxerxes's concern might have been a time of natural disasters in the Middle East, leading the king to believe the people needed to honor the laws of their own gods so they would expect good in their lives.)

3. How might belief that the gods of the nations must be honored or someone would be punished have affected the

---

20 Isbouts, *The Biblical World*, 238.

king and his sons? (The people might have revolted if they blamed the king.)

4. How might human belief play a role in the suffering of the king when nations felt their god was not being honored? (If the people were not enjoying prosperity, they might have felt the king and his family were to blame because their gods were not being honored.)

5. Would an area having no law for its people other than the law of getting along with the conqueror have been a safe place to travel? (Your opinion, please)

6. Artaxerxes commanded Ezra to appoint magistrates and judges to administer justice to the people of the Trans-Euphrates. Why would the administration of justice be important in a battle scared area, full of ruins? (Your opinion, please)

7. Ezra was also to teach the law to those who did not know it and punish those who failed to obey it. Why would that have been necessary? (Your opinion, please. NIVASB Article "The Cylinder," 679)

Ezra's teaching efforts may have had some impact on the city of Jerusalem, because we do know the area around the temple was pretty well inhabited by Jews by the time Nehemiah came to Jerusalem in the twentieth year of Artaxerxes (445 BCE). Ezra left for Jerusalem thirteen years before Nehemiah journeyed there.

Before the temple was finished, when the prophet Haggai was prodding the Jews to finish building it, he said they had paneled the walls in their own houses while the house of the Lord stood unfinished. Paneled walls indicated that they may have built some pretty nice houses for themselves.

After the temple was finished, it was used by Jews living around it. The exiled community apparently built their own houses near the temple during the years there was no repair of the walls of Jerusalem. That left the restored temple and the community attached to the temple open to attack from its many enemies.

Lecture 8

King Artaxerxes I Sends Nehemiah to Rebuild Jerusalem

We need a little background before we move on to Nehemiah's relationship with Artaxerxes. The Persian Empire allowed those deported into Judah by earlier empires to rule the area, which had been ruined by various Middle Eastern conquerors for centuries. Judah was called Trans-Euphrates at this point in history.

Displaced persons of several enemy nations were dropped off in Judah by various conquering armies. These people joined the poorest class of Jews left in Judah when privileged people were deported to Babylon. Babylon's motive for exiling enemies of Judah into their country was to avoid revolt. If the people were from different religions, spoke different languages, considered each other as enemies, it would take more time to establish communication between them.

Some of this local population in the area had managed to work with the Persian Empire to be selected as local governors of the Trans-Euphrates, which included the city of Jerusalem and the province of Judah. When Jewish exiles returned to their homeland to rebuild, they found vassal appointees of Persia were in charge of the area. Those governing officials realized that Jews returning to their homeland might take over the authority they had managed to earn for themselves. Consequently, they opposed rebuilding efforts of the Jews returning from exile in Babylon.

After the temple was rebuilt, work on the city wall was started to protect the temple. Immediately, opposition erupted from local officials—Rehum the high commissioner and Shimshai the secretary. Copies of letters exchanged between them and King Artaxerxes are found in Ezra 4:12–24 (NEB). Parts of these letters appear below.

Be it known to Your Majesty that the Jews who left you and came to these parts have reached Jerusalem and are rebuilding that wicked and rebellious city; they have surveyed the foundation and are completing the walls. Be it known to Your Majesty that, if their city is rebuilt and the walls are completed, they will pay neither general levy, nor poll-tax, nor land-tax, and in the end they will harm the monarchy … You will discover by searching through the annals that this has been a rebellious city, harmful to the monarchy and its provinces and that sedition has long been rife within its walls. (Ezra 4:12-14, 15, NEB)

King Artaxerxes reply was directed to Rehum and Shimshai:

The letter which you sent to me has now been read clearly in my presence. I have given orders and search has been made, and it has been found that the city in question has a long history of revolt against the monarchy and that rebellion and sedition have been rife in it … Therefore issue orders that these men must desist. This city is not to be rebuilt until a decree to that effect is issued by me. See that you do not neglect your duty in this matter, lest more damage and harm be done to the monarchy. (Ezra 4:18-19, 21-22, NEB)

After these letters were sent by Rehum and Shimshai, the governing authorities of Trans-Euphrates to King Artaxerxes, construction was stopped. A footnote to (Ezra 21-23, NIVSB) suggests that the "forcible destruction of these recently rebuilt walls" was the result of the reply from the king.

Scholars agree there was more than one source used in compiling information for the Old Testament book of Nehemiah because both the first and third person is used in the book. Scholars mention the Nehemiah Memoir, an important first person account which contains Nehemiah's interpretation of events which happened during the rebuilding of the wall. Experts, however, believe Ezra compiled the information and authored the book of Nehemiah during the first quarter of the fourth century BCE in Palestine.[21]

The books of Ezra and Nehemiah were two separate compositions that were eventually combined into one book entitled Ezra. The oldest manuscripts of the Septuagint treated them as one book, but Origen (circa AD 165–253) was the first writer to make a distinction between the two which he called 1 Ezra and 2 Ezra. Wycliffe's (1382) and Coverdale's (1835) English translations also separated the two.[22] Presumably later Bible versions adopted Wycliffe and Coverdale's separation of the two books as Ezra and Nehemiah.

Nehemiah's family were exiles in Babylon. Some of the family members apparently did not care to return to Jerusalem when Cyrus the Great decreed that exiles who wished could return to their homeland. Many exiles had made a good life for themselves and had become very prosperous. Nehemiah's family was obviously prominent, as Nehemiah was the cupbearer for King Artaxerxes I. This position would go to an individual who was

---

21 Eerdmans, Nehemiah, Book of, 955
22 "Introduction to Nehemiah," NIVASB.

trusted beyond a doubt, since the cupbearer made certain the king's drink was safe to drink.

We hear from Nehemiah in Chapter 1:

While I was in the citadel of Susa, Hanani, one of my brothers, came from Judah with some other men, and I questioned them about the Jewish remnant that survived the exile, and also about Jerusalem.

They said to me, "Those who survived the exile and are back in the province are in great trouble and disgrace. The wall of Jerusalem is broken down, and its gates have been burned with fire."

When I heard these things, I sat down and wept. For some days I mourned and fasted and prayed before the God of heaven. (Neh. 1:1b-4, NIV)

Nehemiah's brother's comment that "the wall of Jerusalem is broken down and the gates have been burned" probably refers to damage inflicted by governing officials opposed to rebuilding efforts in Jerusalem. This would have happened after King Artaxerxes authorized them to stop Ezra's reconstruction efforts. Scholars believe they spitefully obliterated the walls (see footnote to Ezra 4:21–23 NIVSB).

When it was time for Nehemiah to serve wine for King Artaxerxes, the king asked about his sadness, suggesting that such a change in his behavior must be due to sadness of heart. Even though Nehemiah was afraid, he explained to the king that he was in mourning because the city where his fathers were buried was in ruins and the gates had been destroyed by fire.

The king asked what Nehemiah wished him to do. Nehemiah asked that he be sent to Judah so he could rebuild the city. The king and the queen asked how long the journey would take, and Nehemiah set a time. Taking their interest in his plight as a sign that the hand of his God was upon him, he asked for letters to the governors of the Trans-Euphrates so that he could get to Judah safely, and for a letter to the keeper of the king's forest so he could get timber to repair the gates of the temple and the wall and to build a residence for himself.

The king sent army officers and cavalry to accompany Nehemiah. When he arrived in Judah, he gave the king's letters to the governors of the area. "When Sanballat the Horonite and Tobiah the Ammonite heard about this development, they were very much disturbed that someone had come to promote the welfare of the Israelites (Nehemiah 2:10 NIV).

The work of Rebuilding the Temple at Jerusalem did not go forward after the temple was rebuilt in 516 BCE, because of fierce local opposition and failure to interest various kings of the Persian Empire in the project. The temple stood in the midst of the ruins of Jerusalem surrounded by the leveled city wall, which could not protect Jewish workers from invaders.

The year was 445 BCE when Nehemiah explained Jerusalem's predicament to King Artaxerxes and obtained his permission to rebuild the city and its walls. King Artaxerxes appointed Nehemiah as the governor of Judah for twelve years and sent him on his way with army officers and cavalry to guard him on his journey.[23]

Artaxerxes was the same king who sent Ezra to Jerusalem to look into the state of the law of the God of the Jews. He commanded Ezra to teach the law to his people and to appoint magistrates and judges to bring justice to the people. That was in 458 BCE. It was thirteen years later (445 BCE) when Artaxerxes sent Nehemiah to Jerusalem to rebuild the city wall and the city itself.

---

23 Footnotes to Nehemiah 2:9–10, NIVSB.

Discussion Questions

1. Persians were not worshippers of the God of the Jews. Why might the king have wanted the Jewish Ten Commandments taught in the ruined city of Judah? (Your opinion, please.)

2. Can you think of other concerns besides security? (Your opinion, please.)

3. Realistically, what might concern a king in regard to conquered nations when the king knew very little about the people of the nation and could not visit every area? (Your opinion, please.)

Three groups made reconstruction for Nehemiah and others tough when they tried to rebuild Jerusalem. Even though Nehemiah had authority from Artaxerxes to reconstruct Jerusalem and had been appointed governor of Judah by the king, there was concentrated opposition from officials of Judah.

Sanballat, the Persian appointee for governor of the district of Samaria, including Judah, was Nehemiah's chief opponent. The Samaritans' home base was once the northern kingdom of Israel after they seceded from the House of David. Samaritans were enemies of Jews of the southern kingdom of Israel because Jeroboam, the leader of northern Israel, set up a golden calf in Dan and Bethel for Samaritans to worship so they would not travel to Jerusalem on important religious holidays (1 Kings 12).

Apparently, Sanballat was one of the exiles left in Samaria when the exiled traditional enemies of local populations into each area to avoid any sense of community so revolt against the Assyrian conqueror was avoided.

In addition to the Samaritans, the Persian Empire had given other groups power in the Trans-Euphrates district. One was Esau's clan, the Idumeans, who in ancient history were known as Edomites. Constantly raiding desert nomads chipped away at Edom until they destroyed its government completely. Raiding groups pushed its citizens into the Negev, a desert area that had formerly been southern Judah. People calling themselves Idumeans settled south of Beer-Sheba. Hebron became the chief city of Esau's descendants.

Tobiah was governor of the Persian province of Ammon. During the Persian Empire, their citizens were called Tobiads. As you will remember, Ammon descended from Lot and his younger daughter after the destruction of Sodom and Gomorrah. Lot's daughters, believing the whole earth had been destroyed, intended to save the race by getting their father drunk so they could produce descendants (Genesis 19:30–36). The Ammonites were called Tobiads in Persian times. Descendants of Lot and his older daughter were called Moabites.

The Samaritans, the Edomites, the Ammonites, and the Moabites were all outcasts to the Jews. The Samaritans seceded from the House of David and worshipped two golden calves. The Edomites were descendants of Esau, who sold his birthright for a bowl of lentil stew (Genesis 27). Moabites and Ammonites were descendants of incest. All of these nations were outcasts to the Jews who took pride in the law of their God, the law of Moses. So their presence in the province of Judah as governing authorities under the Persian Empire did not please Jews returning from Babylonian exile or those who had been left among the ruins when Nebuchadnezzar conquered Israel. (See map 6 in the back of the NIVASB to locate Samaria, Edom, Ammon, and Moab.)

When Nehemiah arrived in Jerusalem and looked for people to help repair the wall, those living around the temple became involved in reconstruction. Nehemiah used individuals as well as teams of men to repair specific sections of the wall.

A sample of Nehemiah's savvy as the director of the project is in Nehemiah 3:28–32. He designated the people who lived right in front of each section of the wall that was to be repaired to do the work. That section would help to protect their own property; thus workers would enjoy the fruits of their own labor.

But when Sanballat and Tobiah, the Arabs, the Ammonites and the men of Ashdod heard that the repairs to Jerusalem's wall had gone ahead and that the gaps were being closed, they were very angry. They all plotted together to come and fight against Jerusalem and stir up trouble against it. But we prayed to our God and posted a guard day and night to meet this threat (Nehemiah 4:7–9 NIVASB).

See Neh. Chapters 5, 6 and 7 to follow the following paraphrase.

Some of the Jews said, "There is too much rubble, the workers are afraid. We'll never be able to finish the wall by ourselves." Their enemies warned everyone who would listen, "Before they know what hits them, we will strike them down and put an end to the work." The Jews who lived among our enemies warned the workers what they were saying and that they planned to come from all directions to attack us with swords, spears and bows. But Nehemiah told them, "Don't forget that you serve an awesome God and fight for your families and your homes."

Then Nehemiah stationed half the men to work on building, while the other half stood by holding spears, shields and bows and wearing coats of mail. Supervisors stood behind the workers while men carrying loads had a weapon in one hand and the load in the other. Builders wore a sword as they worked. A trumpeter stayed beside Nehemiah and he told them, "When you hear the trumpet, come running. But remember, our God will fight for us."

So the work went on with half the men holding weapons from dawn until the stars appeared. Nehemiah also told the people, "All men and their servants must stay inside Jerusalem at night, so you can guard at night and build by day." None of us took off our clothes or laid his weapon down, even when going to get water.

The story of how Nehemiah's repair system enabled the wall to be finished, on October 2, 444 BCE,[24] which was in fifty-two days, is told by Nehemiah, chapters 4, 5, and 6. Now the people were safe inside the walls of Jerusalem. People were now able to work, safe from hostility. But much of the city of Jerusalem still lay in ruins.

Nehemiah registered Jews who had returned from exile earlier to join the efforts to rebuild the city of Jerusalem. There was a total of 42,360 Jews. The list of those registered can be read in Nehemiah 7. The leaders of the people settled in Jerusalem. The rest cast lots so that one out of ten people would live in Jerusalem and build their houses there. Some of those registering with Nehemiah signed up for the work of rebuilding the city; others gave money or donated materials, and the work of rebuilding went forward.

Discussion Questions

1. Nehemiah had faith in his God, but other qualities such as realism about the danger his workers were subject to also kept him from losing the battle with his opponents. What were those qualities? (Your opinion, please)

---

24 Footnote to Nehemiah 6:15 NIVSB.

2. Do you think working for Artaxerxes may have helped Nehemiah to be savvy about handling the difficult opposition? (Your opinion, please)

3. Why would working for Artaxerxes help Nehemiah face opposition? (Your opinion, please)

On October 8, 444 BCE, when the temple walls were completed, all the people assembled as one man in the square before the water gate. They told Ezra the scribe to bring out the book of the law of Moses, which the Lord had commanded for Israel.

Ezra the priest brought the Law before the assembly, which was made up of men and women and all who were able to understand. He read it aloud from daybreak until noon as he faced the square before the Water Gate in the presence of the men, women and others who could understand. And all the people listened attentively" (Nehemiah 8:1b, 2–3 NIVASB)

Many Jews listening to Ezra reading had never heard the words of the Holy Scriptures. Ezra, however, was from a family of Levite priests. All the males in his family were priests. His family of exiled priests had helped to put the law of their God together in exile while they were in Babylon. They taught their sons to memorize the law of God as their fathers had done in their homeland. The male children who would also be priests continued to memorize the law throughout all the years of their family's exile, teaching other exiles in Babylon.

People listening to Ezra were profoundly moved by the timeless words, which had been passed down from generation to generation for hundreds of years. Even if children had never heard the words before, they were somehow deeply familiar because of generations of family language patterns. As they followed the readings, they heard familiar expressions used by family members, exhortations to behave in certain ways and punishments for misdeeds if they did not behave. Jewish behavior was deeply rooted in the language in which the law was written.

Discussion Question:

1. What were some of the influences we have studied that helped the holy writings of the Jews to survive siege warfare, destruction of their homeland, and exile in Babylon? (Your opinion, please)

You can read about the impact of these holy writings on all the people who lived in Israel in Nehemiah 8 through 13 which is summarized below.

As Ezra continued to read the law, the people responded with tears. They began to realize their lives fell far short of the words of the law. Jews who had escaped exile because they were uneducated and would not cause trouble for current conquerors had not memorized scripture in school as educated Jews had, so they did not remember the law at all.

While Ezra was praying and confessing, weeping and throwing himself down before the house of God, a large crowd of Israelites—men, women, and children—gathered around him. They too wept bitterly. Then Shecaniah said to Ezra,

We have been unfaithful to our God by marrying foreign women from the peoples around us. But in spite of this, there is still hope for Israel. Now let us make a covenant before our God to send away all these women and their children, in accordance with the counsel of my lord and of those who fear the commands of our God. Rise up; this matter is in your hands. We will support you, so take courage and do it." (Ezra 10:1–4 NIVASB)

Hearing Ezra read commandments against intermarriage with polytheistic peoples, the people realized how far short they had fallen from the commandments of Jewish law. Some polytheistic religions worshiped Molech, the god of the Ammonites, who demanded child sacrifice (Jeremiah 7:30–31 NIV). Also see the footnote to Jeremiah 7:31 (NIVSB).

Many Canaanite religions had fertility cults using male and female shrine prostitutes, associating fertility of crops and animals with human fertility (1 Kings 14:23–24 NIV). Intermarriage involved spouses who were raised to worship gods such as Molech, the god of Ammon; Chemosh, the god of Moab; and other gods of Canaan.

As Ezra read, the Jews began to understand what an impossible situation they were in. They had intermarried for 142 years. Generations of offspring had been raised by polytheistic spouses who could not appreciate the God of the Jews. The years had passed, and even the older generation did not remember the old ways. How would it be possible to wipe out such detestable polytheistic practices and begin again? Tears fell as Ezra read and they realized the distance between their life and the idealistic words that Ezra was reading. A proclamation was then issued throughout Judah and Jerusalem for all the exiles to assemble in Jerusalem. Then Ezra the priest stood up and said to them,

"You have been unfaithful; you have married foreign women, adding to Israel's guilt. Now make confession to the Lord, the God of your fathers and do his will. Separate yourselves from the peoples around you and from your foreign wives." The whole assembly responded with a loud voice: "You are right! We must do as you say but it is the rainy season and we cannot stand outside. Besides, this matter cannot be taken care of in a day or two because we have sinned greatly in this thing." (Ezra 10:7, 10–13 NIVASB)

Even though the people were genuinely repentant about the path their lives had taken, intermarriage was so prevalent that the reform never took root (Nehemiah 13:23; also footnote to Nehemiah 13:23 NIVSB).

Many people were responsible for the preservation of the law of the Jews. Ezra's family of Levite priests preserved the law in exile, passing it down to each generation of priests. For 140-plus years, Ezra and his family of priests taught the law to Jewish exiles in Babylon. Then at Artaxerxes's command, Ezra brought the law to the Jews in Judah who had never left their ancestral land as well as to returned exiles helping to reconstruct Jerusalem.

Artaxerxes I also helped to preserve the law of Moses by sending Ezra to the rebuilt temple to look into the condition of the law of his God. He commanded Ezra to teach the law to the Jews so it would be passed on to future generations. Later he also sent Nehemiah to rebuild the walls of Jerusalem and reconstruct the city. The Persian Empire was actively involved in the reconstruction of war-torn Judah and preservation of the holy scriptures of the Jews.

Conclusion

I reached the conclusion after preparing lectures for *Rebuilding the Temple at Jerusalem* that Israel is a vibrant country today, at least in part because of the ancient Persian Empire's involvement in the restoration of the country.

For more than one hundred years after Cyrus the Great decreed the Jews could return from exile in Babylon to Jerusalem to rebuild the temple, various Persian kings had to take responsibility for the details of rebuilding efforts, or the Jews would not have been successful. Unfriendly exiles who had made a home for themselves among the ruins of Judah—after Nebuchadnezzar destroyed the temple—did not welcome returning Jews hoping to reclaim their land. They opposed rebuilding efforts at every stage of reconstruction. Only with the help of various kings of the Persian Empire were they able to complete the restoration.

In the modern world of huge political and religious divides, it is difficult to lay aside the issues that separate us and concentrate on the similarities that unite us. A look back in history reminds us that we have cooperated in the past and that cooperation in the future is essential if the world is to survive.

When lone terrorists anywhere on earth can take command of a weapon that can bring down airliners flying seven miles high, we must reconsider old rivalries. Justice is important to everyone, and chronic injustice can fuel extremism.

Bibliography

Bertman, Stephen. *Handbook to Life in Ancient Mesopotamia.* Facts on File, Inc., NYC, 2003.

Blake, E. C., and A. G. Edmonds. *Biblical Sites in Turkey*, 5th ed. Istanbul, Turkey: RedhousePress, 1994.

Campbell; Moyers. *The Power of Myth.* New York: Doubleday, 1988.

DeHaan, M. R. *The Jew and Palestine in Prophecy.* Grand Rapids, Michigan: Zondervan, 1950.

Freedman, David, ed. *Eerdmans Dictionary of the Bible.* Grand Rapids, Michigan: Wm. Eerdmans Pub., 2000.

Gardiner, Joseph, ed. *Atlas of the Bible.* Pleasantville, New York: Reader's Digest Association, 1981.

Hicks, Jim A. *A Soaring Spirit.* Alexandria, VA:Time, 1987. *Holy Bible.* King James Version. Grand Rapids:Zondervan, 2008

Hubbard, R. Dean. *Letter to Israel, God's Countdown for Mankind.* Lake Mary, Florida: Creation House, 2006.

Isbouts, Jean-Pierre. *The Biblical World: An Illustrated Atlas.* Washington, DC: National Geographic, 2007.

Tanakh The Holy Scriptures, The New JPS Translation. Philadelphia: Jewish Publication Society, 1985.

Nelson's Complete Book of Bible Maps and Charts. Nashville, Tennessee: Thomas Nelson Pub., 1996.

New International Version Archaeological Study Bible. Grand Rapids, Michigan: Zondervan, 2005.

New International Version Study Bible. Grand Rapids, Michigan: Zondervan, 1995.

The New English Bible. New York: Oxford University Press, Corrected Impression, 1972.

New Larousse Encyclopedia of Mythology. New York: Crown Publishers, 1986.

New Revised Standard Version with Apocrypha. Nashville, Tennessee: Thomas Nelson, 1989.

New Testament and Psalms: An Inclusive Version. New York: Oxford University Press, 1995.

Pagels, Elaine. *Revelations, Visions, Prophecy, and Politics.* New York: Penguin Books, 2012.

Reader's Digest Complete Guide to the Bible. Pleasantville, New York: Reader's Digest Association, 1998.

Shanks, Hershel, ed. *Ancient Israel: A Short History from Abraham to the Roman Destruction of the Temple.* Washington, DC: Prentice-Hall, 2008.

The Living Bible. Wheaton, Illinois: Tyndale House Publishers, 1971.

Wright, Ernest G., ed. *Great People of the Bible and How They Lived.* Pleasantville, New York: Reader's Digest Association, 1979.

Yenen, Serif. *Turkish Odyssey: A Cultural Guide to Turkey.* Istanbul, Turkey: Meander Publishing, 2001.

www.ingramcontent.com/pod-product-compliance
Lightning Source LLC
LaVergne TN
LVHW040158080526
838202LV00042B/3221